S0-FQW-766

Handling the

PAIN

While Holding to the

PROMISE

RON WALLACE

Copyright © 2018 Ron Wallace
ISBN: 978-1-940359-70-0
Library of Congress Control Number: 2018945163
Published in the United States of America

All rights reserved as permitted under the U. S. Copyright Act of 1976. No part of this publication may be reproduced, distributed, or transmitted in any form or by any means, or stored in a database or retrieval system, without the expressed written permission of the author and publisher.

Unless otherwise identified, all Scripture quotations have been taken from the *NEW AMERICAN STANDARD BIBLE*, Copyright © 1960, 1962,1963,1968,1971,1972,1973,1975,1977,1995 by The Lockman Foundation. Used by permission.

Scriptural quotation marked (KJV) are taken from the *King James Bible.*

Scriptural quotation marked (NLT) are taken from *the Holy Bible, New Living Translation*, copyright 1996. Used by permission of the Tyndale House Publishers, Inc. Wheaton, Illinois 60189. All rights reserved.

Scripture marked (GWT) is taken from *GOD'S WORD*, © 1995 God's Word to the Nations. Used by permission of Baker Publishing Group.

Bedford, Texas
BurkhartBooks.com

DEDICATION

This book is dedicated to everyone who continues to experience pain while waiting for God's promise to be fulfilled in your life.

I know your pain, but God knows it more because He knows you. You continue to believe His promise. He continues to believe in you.

God sees each time you fall. He doesn't see you as a failure. He sees your mistakes but you are not a mistake.

Abba Father still holds to His promise. Keep holding on to your hope. This book was written to give you hope, the only thing that may be left.

CONTENTS

DEDICATION

THE PREMISE   7
THE PERSON   13
THE PROMISE   21
THE PROCESS   29
THE PLIGHT   37
THE PAIN   43
THE POSSESSION   51
THE PERCEPTION   57
THE POSTSCRIPT   61

ABOUT THE AUTHOR

THE PREMISE

The premise of this book is about a man named Caleb who saw firsthand how the promise of God brought about pain. No assembly of people experienced as much pain than the children of Israel while waiting for God's promise to get them to their Promised Land.

Generations were born and died while God's promise remained unfulfilled. What happened to His promise? Why all this pain?

God knew of their upcoming pain before they crossed the river into the land promised more than 500 years earlier.

He also knew of your current pain before you were created. But more importantly, He knows it now.

I've experienced some very deep pain in my life. A special needs child was born to us while I was attending seminary. A few years later my beautiful wife, Dianne, died at 47 years old while in the middle of parenting three children.

Our special needs child and my wife's deaths brought about a lot of questions that were never fully answered. I no longer question but accept them as part of the process we call "life."

It's not so much what happens to you in life, but how you handle what happens to you.

Life is not what others say while you **live here**. It's not even about what they say when you **leave here**. Instead, life is all about what God says when you **arrive there**.

People on earth soon forget your accomplishments. Records set will later be shattered. Money accumulated will all be left behind. Your name will eventually no longer be spoken by others. Those who remembered you will soon no longer be here to remember.

But how will God remember you?

You've messed up at times in your life like everyone else. You may feel you have messed up your entire life. How does God see you at this moment based upon how you've lived your life up to this point?

Complete the following sentence in your mind.

God sees me as a person who _____.

It's not about the size of your mistakes. It's about the size of your God. If you have experienced **pain** when you thought you should be experiencing God's **promise**, this book is for you.

Pain is sometimes experienced while waiting on a promise of God to be fulfilled.

An adage in life is "No Pain. No Gain." Sometimes it feels better to accept "No Pain. No Pain." Why experience the pain when it may not be worth the gain?

Pain is experienced at birth and usually accompanies death. Life cannot be lived without pain because of the fallen world where we currently live. You cannot escape pain in life until you have escaped life.

This book does not deal with the topic of why bad things happen to good people. Then one would also have to wrestle with the subject of why good things happen to bad people.

Maybe you don't deserve some of the bad things you have already experienced. And then you may not deserve some of the good things coming your way either.

Life is influenced by the way you think and approach it. This book can assist and encourage you to pursue what God has promised and planned for your life.

The human tendency is to ultimately become what you imagine or image yourself as being. A person seems to act in response to one's self-image. It works best when combined with God's Word and by remembering you are created in the image of God.

One of the most important take-aways from this book is to have a belief system in place that will impact your life in a positive and meaningful way.

Nothing is recorded in the Bible about anything Caleb did or said that caused his delay of experiencing God's promise for his life. But there was a delay. And there was pain.

You will see how he maintained his focus as he patiently waited 40 additional years after God was ready to give what was promised to the children of Israel.

What is a promise in your life that has become painful while waiting for God to release it? A lesson can be learned while you read about Caleb advancing in years as the clock of life was running out on his life.

Caleb had a personal belief system that made him different. It helped him through the dark period when the Israelites were right on the edge of seeing God's promise fulfilled after 400 years of silence.

Caleb's way of believing can be described as a "credo." You may be more familiar with the term, "creed," but they are different.

CREED – a shared belief statement with others that is considered more religious in nature.

THE APOSTLES' CREED AND NICENE CREED

The Apostles' Creed was not produced by the apostles, but rather summarized their teachings. It contains an overview of their faith and is considered one of the oldest creeds in the Christian church.

The Nicene Creed is a doctrine used as a Christian liturgy mainly about God and the Trinity. It is widely accepted by most major entities of the Christian faith.

CREDO – a Latin word meaning, "I believe," is more of a personal statement. It is a belief system about one's faith and obedience. It is not necessarily bound to a group.

> *You are the Christ, the Son of the living God.*
> Matthew 16:16

This was Peter's personal statement about his belief in Jesus and can be referred to as *Peter's Credo*.

Caleb's Credo is his belief system about a certain aspect of his life and his belief in a living and true God. It will appear at the end of certain chapters.

That will be followed by a *Personal Credo*, one you can use or modify to help you process God's promises, especially the ones accompanied by pain.

They will also appear once again at the end of the last chapter with suggestions about how to implement them in your daily living.

Next is the first credo based upon this chapter, The Premise.

CALEB'S CREDO – THE PREMISE

Caleb believed God would not forget him or the promise made generations earlier. He stayed positive even though the process was painful.

Caleb believed he had a different belief system that made him different.

Caleb believed he was called for such a time as this in Israel's history.

PERSONAL CREDO – THE PREMISE

I believe God created me with a calling for such a time as this. He knew me before I was born and knows my pain now.

I believe God's promise is coming my way because I choose to believe in a different way.

I believe God's mercy will accompany me through the dark nights of the soul.

THE PERSON

*But my servant Caleb has a different attitude
than the others have ….*
                                        Numbers 14:24 (NLT)

Caleb was not of Jewish descent but was an Edomite. His bloodline went through the lineage of Esau rather than Jacob. He was the son of Jephunneh the Kenizzite which meant he was born outside the family of the Israelites.

Caleb was born as an Egyptian slave where he was in bondage to the pharaoh and worked alongside other fellow sufferers for 38 years until released.

He was adopted as a member of the tribe of Judah where he became a warrior and later their leader as one of the 12 tribes of Israel.

Caleb may not have been the one the Israelites were looking to lead them. His pedigree left something to be desired. But his desire was to follow God and others later followed because of that desire.

CALEB HAD A PROMISE

There was a promise earlier made by God to Abraham that his descendants would be granted a land described as flowing with milk and honey. The Israelites lived for that promise. Many died waiting for the promise to be fulfilled.

Caleb kept God's promise as his focal point as he remembered and reminded others of His promise. His comfort zone centered around that promise and sometimes found himself more in the minority than the majority.

Caleb was one of the 12 spies who went on a reconnaissance mission to the land of the giants. Ten of them collectively feared the enemy which made them the majority.

The size of the enemy didn't matter to Caleb. It was the size of his God that counted. That familiar outlook kept him in the column of the minority.

CALEB HAD A PURPOSE

God created Caleb who was certainly wired differently than most people around him. There was a specific calling for a specific time in history.

There was no one like Caleb and never will be again. That's why we are made so differently because each of us has a specific purpose. The psalmist described how we are created so uniquely different:

You made all the delicate, inner parts of my body
and knit me together in my mother's womb.
Thank you for making me so wonderfully complex!
Your workmanship is marvelous—how well I know it.
You watched me as I was being formed in utter seclusion,
as I was woven together in the dark of the womb.
Psalm 139:13-15 (NLT)

Jesus' life was the perfect example of fulfilling His purpose in life. Think about it in the following way:

Jesus had no misgivings → only a mission

Jesus had no status → only a statement

Jesus had no Board → only a belief

How could Jesus say *It is finished* when:

- the hungry needed to be fed?
- the sick needed to be healed?
- the unlearned needed to learn?
- the unlovely needed to be loved?

- Jesus knew His mission had been completed.

- Jesus never made a mistake about His mission.

- Jesus never missed the direction of His mission.

One of the ways that may help you determine your purpose in life is by your gifting. A specific calling calls for specific giftings. Some call it talents; others refer to it as gifts.

Matthew 25:14-30 is the parable of talents told by Jesus. It may refer to money, but it also can be equated with your giftings. The story unfolds about a man who goes on a journey and entrusts his property to those who worked for him.

He gave one worker five talents, to another two talents, and to one he gave one. There was a reason for the way the talents were distributed. Each one received according to his ability.

God is the <u>distributor</u> of the gifts.

God determines the <u>distribution</u>.

There is a <u>difference</u> in the distribution.

It's not so much about how MANY gifts are entrusted to you, but how they are MANAGED

CALEB HAD A PASSION

Caleb set the standard for a life with passion. He had certain goals in life, but his life was not just about goals; it was about God. He kept his eye on God and he also kept it on the goal God created for him. That was Caleb's passion.

What does your Passion Meter indicate? Ask yourself the following questions:

Do I enjoy getting up every morning?

Do I say, "Good morning, God" or "Good God, it's morning?"

Do I think about "Thanks" or "Tasks?"

Do I think about my purpose in life every day?

Do I enjoy laughter on a regular basis?

Do I smile most of the time?

Do I have a daily quiet time?

Do I "re-create" myself during recreation time?

Think of your gifting as you read about Caleb. And then do an inventory check to determine the reasons how and why God has gifted you. Your gifting gives you a sense of purpose and fulfillment when you are performing certain tasks with certain gifts.

Fredrick Buechner explained it in terms of gifting and gladness:

What Makes Us Gladdest

The voice we should listen to most as we choose a vocation
is the voice that we might think we should listen to the
least, and that is the voice of our own gladness.
What can we do that makes us the gladdest,
What can we do that leaves us with the strongest sense
of sailing due north and of peace,
Which is much of what gladness is?

Is it making things with our hands
out of wood, or stone, or paint or canvas?
Or is it making something we hope,
like truth, out of words?
Or is it making people laugh
or weep in a way that cleanses the spirit?

I believe that if it is a thing that makes us truly glad,
Then it is a good thing and it is our thing, and it is the
calling voice that we were made to answer with our lives.

Life was too precious for you to wander aimlessly through it, so you did some strategic planning. You set goals. You wrote objectives. You developed a personal mission statement for your life.

Then something happened. A career ending injury halted a promising professional career. The financial means needed for higher education never came through.

The family business you counted on is now corporately owned. Your retirement plan is no longer part of the new employer's plan.

Your marriage may have ended on the rocks, a marriage you thought was founded on the Rock. The birth of a child blind-sided you with more responsibility. Your dreams have finally become that—only dreams. You planned your life. What happened was not what you planned.

You were a plan in God's mind before you ever had a plan in your mind. Your uniqueness is not because of your plan. It was part of His plan from the very beginning.

Maybe you don't know where you are in life right now. You may not even know what life is about. Caleb knew his calling. God knew Caleb's commitment.

You may not know your calling. You're not even sure about your commitment. But God knows your heart; He also knows your indiscretions and your insecurities.

Life is not always measured in terms of duration or years. That refers to life as a "quantity." There is also a "quality" of life. Think of what's ahead. Don't think about what's behind you.

Life is not measured just in terms of quantity or duration. Rather it's about quality or donation.

What you __are__ is more important than what you __were__.
What you __can be__ is more important than what you __are__.

Brent Barlow

CALEB'S CREDO – THE PERSON

Caleb believed he was to follow God as God followed up on His promise about the Promised Land. He knew his calling and God knew his commitment.

Caleb believed he could overcome any problem with God's power. He exercised his faith when facing fear and simply believed what God said.

Caleb believed God's promise and made it his focal point in life. He believed with a passion about the purpose of God as well as God's place for His people.

PERSONAL CREDO – THE PERSON

I believe God created me uniquely different with specific giftings that grant me a sense of purpose.

I believe God had a plan in mind from the very beginning before I ever had a plan in mind.

I believe God will help me overcome any obstacle that may block any opportunity He makes available.

THE PROMISE

It began with a promise made by God to Abraham and his descendants 500 years before Moses, Joshua, and Caleb came on the scene.

The promise was to one day be able to possess a land known as Canaan, often referred to as the Promised Land. The promise had very few details:

> *Go out from your land to the land I will show you.*
> Genesis 12:1

Abraham had to leave what he thought was his future. He associated his future with his surroundings. He saw his future as far as he could see but was unable to see what God was seeing.

Abraham's descendants settled in Egypt after a famine drove them to that location. The descendants multiplied greatly and were later subjected to bondage when a new pharaoh came to the throne in Egypt.

> *And the sons of Israel sighed because of the bondage,*
> *and they cried out; and their cry for help*
> *because of their bondage rose up to God.*
> *So God heard their groaning;*
> *and remembered His covenant with Abraham, Isaac,*
> *and Jacob. And God saw the sons of Israel,*
> *and God took notice of them.*
> Exodus 2:23-25

A MENTOR FOR CALEB

Moses was God's chosen leader to later lead the children of Israel out of bondage and slavery. It was at this stage in Moses' life where he became a major player when God initiated a move among His people.

Forty years earlier Moses had a turn of events that caused him to turn away from leadership. Moses was cut off from his past and couldn't see anything in his future.

He was found watching over sheep he didn't even own. It was on that backside of the wilderness where Moses experienced God once again. It began with that promise made by God to Abraham.

It can also begin with a promise from God to you. You don't know if it means staying where you are or going to a different place or position in life.

Like Abraham, God may have only said, "I will show you," but hasn't given you traveling directions. The unknown will sometimes cause a person to become unwilling to "go" so God can "show."

You may be in a place, like Moses, where you prefer not to be, and no one wants to be there with you. It's become a wilderness experience in your mind and in your life.

You have no direction because there seems to be no direction for you to go. You feel like giving up on yourself because you sense God may have given up on you long ago.

Just as Moses experienced God once again, it could also be on the backside of a desert where your wilderness wandering has taken you. That may allow you to experience God once again.

It may be where God took you rather than you just ending up there. He knows where you are and where He can use you. God will take you where you need to go, even though you feel like you're going nowhere.

Moses also provided a degree of mentoring to Caleb during this time since he rose rather quickly through the ranks. God selected the mentor for Caleb because when one chooses, it sometimes is not the best choice.

A mentor should be a person who is experienced and a trusted advisor. Moses may not have been a hands-on mentor where he micromanaged the activities of Caleb but was available for providing advice or direction indirectly.

You may prefer someone like yourself. That may become more of a liability than an asset. A mentor is not just about relationships. There are certain qualifications that mentors need for certain types of mentoring.

You don't go looking for a mentor. A mentor usually finds you. Moses was aware that Caleb and Joshua were the only two spies who came back with a positive report. He must have seen something that caught his attention.

There is no indication Caleb sought out Moses to mentor him. But the tribe of Judah must have seen something in Caleb when he surfaced to become their leader.

Caleb saw how God selected Moses to lead the people's exodus. He watched how God used Moses to send the plagues that took their toll on the Egyptians. Caleb was an eyewitness to the following nasty turn of events:

1. Plague of Blood
2. Plague of Frogs
3. Plague of Lice/Gnats
4. Plague of Flies
5. Plague of Livestock
6. Plague of Boils
7. Plague of Hail
8. Plague of Locusts
9. Plague of Darkness
10. Plague of Firstborn Deaths

You wonder how anyone could not believe or trust in such a mighty God. It was God's own people, the Israelites, who lost sight of their God.

A MIRACLE FOR CALEB

Caleb watched as God's promise to His people faced a water problem. The Promised Land was ahead of them and the Egyptian army behind them in heavy pursuit. A body of water known as the Red Sea was in between.

If God didn't come through, His children were through. Caleb watched to see how God was going to use Moses, the one called earlier to be the leader of God's people.

God would <u>deliver</u> the people.
Moses only had to <u>direct</u> the people.

The children of Israel were standing at the edge of the Red Sea. They began to hear a violent wind growing. It grew louder and stronger by the hour.

The wind became so violent that the elements of nature could not withstand its force, not even the waters of the Red Sea.

Imagine the look on the faces of family members as they huddled together, unable to talk or even hear each other because of the powerful wind.

Caleb may have wondered what Moses was thinking just before Moses raised his arms to part the Red Sea as God instructed. He was watching just like the others, but his thoughts were unlike the others.

Caleb had a different attitude that allowed him to anticipate something differently. He saw the water problem up close and personal.

Before the problem, there was a promise by the same God who brought suffering and death to their enemies. He promised deliverance, but it seemed as if the people kept delaying because they kept disbelieving.

A miracle was literally taking place as the waters of the Red Sea opened before them. God was beginning to reveal Himself once again to His chosen people after 400 years of silence.

God was providing an escape route from their enemy. They were on their way to a new beginning, a Promised Land that was promised to their forefathers.

You waited for what seemed an eternity for this time in your life. You were beginning to experience a miracle on your journey. God was finally moving you forward.

Then you realize it's taking much longer than you anticipated. You hear the enemy fast approaching behind you. Satan has a way of showing up right after a miracle.

**Just when you think you're an <u>overcomer</u>,
Satan tries to <u>overcome</u> you.**

God told His children what He was going to do, but He didn't tell their enemy. When the enemy is closing in on you, then you'll know you're closing in on a miracle. When God takes care of you, He'll also take care of your enemies.

Instead of anticipating what miracles God wants to do in your life, you may be wondering what you will do if God doesn't perform a miracle. How you approach a miracle sometimes determines how God approaches you.

God wants your expectation to rise in the same way Caleb's anticipation rose when he saw Moses raise his arms.

Until you come to the realization you have no other choice, your mind may continue to search for other choices. Choose God as your only choice and He may choose that moment for your miracle.

The two most important days in your life are the day you were born and the day you find out why.
Mark Twain

You know the day you were born. But maybe you don't know where you are today in relation to God's promises to you.

You were born for such a time as this because God's calling is accompanied with your gifting. And your gifting is in conjunction with your purpose and passion.

Sometimes when God begins to fulfill His promise, it may not initially be what you anticipated. You think there must be a mistake and you feel you are being misdirected.

Maybe that promise died in you when you experienced one of life's roadblocks or dead end. You wonder if this was all there was to life.

God is omniscient, meaning He is all-knowing. He knows everything that was known and knows all that will even be known. There is nothing He had to learn, and nothing takes Him by surprise.

Behind each of God's promises is a process. For the promise to be finalized, the process must be fulfilled. He may not have given you all the information that encompasses the process, but only the promise.

God is the one that gave you the earlier promise and He's the one that knows when it will be fulfilled. And that's a promise.

CALEB'S CREDO - THE PROMISE

Caleb believed in the leadership of Moses and how God's power came through Moses as the Egyptians couldn't escape the horrific plagues from God.

Caleb believed God used Moses to solve the water problem with the Red Sea.

Caleb believed with a different attitude that allowed him to anticipate something different coming from God.

PERSONAL CREDO – THE PROMISE

I believe my life began with a promise from God.

I believe when God takes care of me, He also take cares of my enemies.

I believe God is helping me through this wilderness experience and is moving from bondage to blessings.

THE PROCESS

The promise doesn't always synchronize with the process since God has His own timeframe. Even though you're <u>about time</u>, God is <u>above time</u>.

**When God renders you a <u>promise</u>,
He will also reveal the <u>process</u>.**

You may feel you are out of your comfort zone but at least you do have a sense of movement taking place. Even that initial move can be a part of God's bigger move in your life.

There may be something within the process that doesn't seem to be moving. And there comes that dreaded word, "delay." You don't understand when it happens.

Sometimes you feel there is no way you can encounter another delay because the clock is still running, and you are running out of time.

God has all the time in the world and in heaven.

The delay may only be a short hesitancy. And then it could be a major braking that stalls in the middle of nowhere.

The Israelites were now in the middle of nowhere. They were between Egypt, the land of bondage, and the land of Canaan, the land of bounty.

The children of God had been freed from the bondage of Egypt's pharaoh after 400 years of slavery and brutal taskmasters. God sent ten plagues upon the land and the inhabitants of Egypt.

The ruler released the Israelites from bondage and then thought he made a bad decision. But that was too bad. The soldiers and their horses drowned while pursuing those God had just extended freedom.

The Israelites were just on the outskirts of their prized possession. Moses sent 12 spies, one from each tribe, to search out the long-awaited destination of Canaan. He wanted a report on four things:

(1) the <u>fortification</u> of the land;
(2) the <u>fruit</u> of the land;
(3) the <u>formation</u> of the land;
(4) the <u>features</u> of the land dwellers.

They waited for the spies to return. It took 40 days; it seemed like a long time. But that was nothing compared to the 400 years of the earlier waiting.

Many people are looking for direction in life today. They know life goes on, but don't know where to go. They don't want to enter the unknown without knowing what is ahead.

A scouting report from someone who went ahead earlier could help them determine whether to move ahead or maintain their position.

Moses' spies brought back a sampling of the fruit for others to taste of the bountiful blessings that awaited them. Then came the report:

(1) The fortified cities could be seen from a distance;
(2) The fruit of the land had to be tasted to be believed;
(3) The formation of the land was amazingly beautiful, especially the hill country of Hebron.

The good news was barely stated when the following bad news swallowed up the remaining reporting session.

So they gave out to the sons of Israel a bad report
of the land which they had spied out.

Numbers 13:32

(4) The features of the land dwellers were a sight to see, even from a distance. The spies' faith was immediately dwarfed when they saw the size of those possessing the land earlier promised.

They earlier <u>tasted the grapes</u>
Now they were to be <u>tested by the giants</u>.

Caleb saw it coming even though he saw the same things reported by the ten other spies. Joshua and Caleb saw the inhabitants differently and knew God's promise was about to derail.

A decision is usually based upon a physiological reaction formed by one's frame of reference in response to a possible harmful event or a threat to one's survival.

Frame of Reference:
A specific set of beliefs used to make a decision.

The response is framed as <u>Fight or Flight</u> where your body prepares to exert energy to either fight or take flight. You make one of two choices. You confront the threat or the person and deal with it OR remove yourself as far away as quickly as possible.

The children of Israel had been in bondage 400 years. God delivered the children of Israel from physical bondage, but they were still in bondage from a spiritual perspective. They developed a **paralysis from analysis** by over analyzing the situation. Over analyzing or over thinking can result in making no decision or taking no action.

Caleb heard the **flight** response in the report of the spies. He saw the same giants, but that wasn't a concern. Caleb's problem was with the ten spies.

They lied! They said all the people were giants. That was not true, only a few. But the few were enough to give a bad report to the many.

Caleb needed to grab the crowd's immediate attention and draw their focus back to the process. Caleb quieted the people and said:

We should by all means go up and take possession of it, for we shall surely overcome it.

Numbers 13:30

There was a different <u>frame of reference</u> for Caleb because he saw it differently. Caleb remembered what God told Moses earlier:

I have come down to deliver them from the power of the Egyptians, and to bring them to a good and spacious land, to a land flowing with milk and honey ...

Exodus 3:8

The spies whipped the multitude into a frenzy by saying all was doom and gloom. No Canaan for them because it was already occupied.

Their report made no mention of the Lord. Caleb's report mentioned the Lord's name several times. He was passionate because he saw the potential.

Passion is not <u>hoping</u> your plans happen.
Passion is <u>helping</u> your plans happen.

Caleb saw the same giants and stated the facts in his report. But he didn't avoid the problem. The giants were big, but his God was bigger.

Caleb wanted the very best and believed God would give it to him. He didn't listen to others because he didn't want to live in the past. Caleb was ready to move into his future residence.

How passionate were the ones listening to the false report about their possibilities? They were passionate enough to tell others to pick up rocks and stone Joshua and Caleb.

Often the crowd does not recognize a leader
until he has gone, and then they build a monument
for him with the stones they threw at him in life.
Oswald Sanders

Leaders are neither infallible nor invincible. They are humans like all of us, but they must assume more responsibility and be held to a higher standard.

An applicable rule while going through the process is the trust factor. When broken, it will ultimately lead to other things such as misdirection and even misfortune; it is very difficult to recover.

The spies lied and later died. Their report caused a generation of people to die in the wilderness who would never reach their destiny.

Sin can cause you to spiritually die
and never reach your destiny.

A decision you are facing may not doom an entire nation, but it may affect your family, possibly your business, or even the people of the city where you reside. It will affect you and could later reflect upon you.

You would feel much better if you could just get a sign or a word from God. A miracle at this moment may feel more appropriate. If you could just get something from God, it would make the decision much easier.

God has given you something. He has given you His presence. He is present at this very moment in your very own life if you have accepted His Son into your life.

God's Spirit is in you. Rather than looking outward for a sign, listen inward to His Spirit. Now may be the time for you to make that decision and move forward. What do you see in your future? Is it grapes or giants?

**What you think is ahead of you is
what you believe is in your future.**

Sometimes you feel as if you can only stand and look. You know what you want. You know where to find it. You also know what you need to do.

There are many obstacles in life and some of them are still ahead. God has prepared a life of abundance for you, even if others are telling you the odds are against you for such a life.

God may be waiting for you to make a move, so He can make His next move.

CALEB'S CREDO - THE PROCESS

Caleb believed what God promised earlier and that gave him a different frame of reference.

Caleb believed his God was bigger than his enemies and didn't avoid the problem.

Caleb believed God would give him the very best and anticipated God's blessings.

PERSONAL CREDO – THE PROCESS

I believe God has a process for each of His promises. Each process must be fulfilled for the promises to be finalized.

I believe God has a timeframe for me and He is always on time as each promise becomes a reality.

I believe God can bring about the needed miracle at this time in my life.

THE PLIGHT

A "plight" is defined as a dangerous or difficult situation where a person or group of people sometimes find themselves.

Then all the congregation lifted up their voices and cried, and the people wept that night … So they said one to another, "Let us appoint a leader and return to Egypt."

Numbers 14:1,4

The Israelites, who had been in captivity for over 400 years, were now a free people. They no longer experienced a physical captivity but were now beginning to experience a mental captivity.

They'd just received a briefing from the spies who had returned from their reconnaissance mission with a less than sterling report. The minds of the former slaves became imprisoned with negative thoughts and never-ending questions about the condition they found themselves.

When you question God, you're not looking for an explanation from God. You may be looking for an excuse to argue with Him.

The people of God knew why they'd been set free. They were God's children, His chosen people. They weren't looking for an explanation about their recent freedom. What they wanted now was an excuse to argue about their present condition.

There were three things the spies reported that caused the promise of God to be postponed. The first was the **strength of the enemy**.

> *But the other men who had explored the land*
> *with them disagreed. "We can't go up against them!*
> *They are stronger than we are."*
>
> Numbers 13:31 (NLT)

They talked about the strength of the enemy and yet never mentioned the strength of their God in the report. How could such "brave" men forget the way God earlier displayed His strength against the Egyptian army? They were earlier drowned and defeated.

The second thing the spies reported on was the **strife among the enemy**.

> *So they spread this bad report about the land among the*
> *Israelites: "The land we traveled through and explored will*
> *devour anyone who goes to live there…"*
>
> Numbers 13:32 (NLT)

The land was very rich and fertile; it was described as flowing with milk and honey. How could land with such a description be one that devours the people?

The fertility of the land caused the inhabitants to fight over the land. The desirability created a division between the land dwellers and the land dividers.

The third thing the spies reported on was the **size of the enemy**.

> *We even saw giants there, the descendants of Anak.*
> *Next to them we felt like grasshoppers,*
> *and that's what they thought, too!*
>
> Numbers 13:33 (NLT)

The spies used the word "grasshoppers" as a self-description. That's the way they felt the enemy saw them because of the way they saw themselves.

People see you the way you see yourself.

If you have a lot of confidence, people see you as a confident person. If you have a lot of insecurities, people see you as an insecure person.

> *The one thing you cannot take away from me is*
> *the way I choose to respond to what you do to me.*
> *The last of one's freedom is to choose one's*
> *attitude in any given circumstance.*
>
> Victor Frankl

Victor Frankl was an Austrian neurologist and psychiatrist that survived the Holocaust. He described his time in the Nazi concentration camps in a best-selling book, *Man's Search for Meaning*.

Dr. Frankl points out that if you don't have hope, which he describes as the future, then death will soon come.

He described how prisoners in the concentration camps who lost faith in the future became doomed.

When a day begins with a **doubt**, it usually ends with a **delay**. If you really don't expect anything good to happen to you during the day, you probably won't be disappointed.

God is not disappointed in you, but disappointed because the good things He had for you that day will be delayed.

Your mind is flooded with thoughts the moment your eyes open and your feet touch the floor. Before you listen to what God is saying He can do, the enemy reminds you what you can't do.

Along with unstable thoughts comes an unstable day. You try to believe but eventually the waves of doubt sink His promises you wanted to hold on to that day.

You even recalled God's promises and testimonies by others how God showed His love. You just can't seem to personally experience this yourself. Is it God or is it you?

When you lie down again at night, you pray to God to let tomorrow be different. You don't want it to be the same life you experienced today. Deep down inside you wonder if He really cares or if anything will really change.

When your day begins, begin by believing. Another day means another opportunity to experience His love and blessings custom ordered from above for you. You don't have to live another day for no reason. Every day is a special day.

One day you'll come face to face with the Lord. When you look into His eyes, will you be thanking Him for the blessings He gave you? Or will you be thinking about all those you didn't receive because of the many days that began with doubt?

Caleb refused to live such a life with such doubt, but rather acknowledged God's calling on his life and lived it with passion. Caleb's purpose was to follow a belief system that God would lead His people to the Land of Promise because God promised it.

The plight eventually brought much pain to God's chosen people because of their disobedience. There are times when God's promises often result in pain. But Caleb knew he was called for such a time.

God has called you for such as time as this—this time today.

CALEB'S CREDO - THE PLIGHT

Caleb believed God's calling was on his life and lived it with passion.

Caleb believed his purpose in following God was to help others who also followed.

Caleb believed he was to live his life with no doubts and with hope.

PERSONAL CREDO - THE PLIGHT

I believe God's promise is on the way, even if there is a delay. I begin each day by believing.

I believe God gives me the opportunity to experience His love and blessings that make each day special.

I believe God's strength is mightier than the strength of my enemy who will experience defeat, even at this moment.

THE PAIN

*For the sons of Israel walked forty years in the wilderness
until all the nation, that is the men of war
who came out of Egypt, perished because
they did not listen to the voice of the Lord.*

Joshua 5:6

God made a promise to His people. There was a process in place to provide them land flowing with milk and honey. But instead of <u>invading</u> the land, they began <u>evading</u> it.

It was currently occupied by giants. Caleb reminded the people even though the giants were big, their God was bigger. They chose to ignore God's process and Caleb's report.

**You can <u>include</u> God's process and watch it <u>unfold.</u>
OR You can <u>ignore</u> God's process and watch it <u>unravel</u>.**

No more fulfilling the earlier promise of possessing the land was expected for those men 20 years and older, except Joshua and Caleb. The inaccurate report of the 10 spies and the indecisiveness of the people resulted in pain.

Fear can spread like the plague, and so it was with the Israelites. God called His own people evil and said any fighting men over 20-years-old would die in the wilderness because of their unfaithfulness.

And the 10 spies who brought back a bad report would die by a plague. Immediate occupancy was no longer an option for those who opted out of invading the land.

These were the same people who saw the Red Sea stand wall to wall for them to pass through on dry ground. The

43

journey to the Promised Land was to take only about 14 days. That was no longer possible.

**Unsuccessful people make decisions
based upon <u>where they are</u>.
Successful people make decisions
based upon <u>where they want to be</u>.**

HOW DID THE ASSEMBLED PEOPLE REACT?

*Then all the congregation lifted their voices and cried,
and the people wept that night. And all the sons of Israel
grumbled against Moses and Aaron ....*
Numbers 14:1

HOW DID MOSES AND AARON REACT?

*Then Moses and Aaron fell on their faces in the presence of all
the assembly of the congregation of the sons of Israel.*
Numbers 14:5

HOW DID JOSHUA AND CALEB REACT?

*And Joshua the son of Nun and Caleb, the son of Jephunneh,
of those who spied out the land, tore their clothes.*
Numbers 14:6

HOW DID GOD REACT?

*How long will this people spurn Me? And how long will
they not believe in Me, despite all the signs which I have
performed in their midst?*
Numbers 14:11

Moses told the Israelites if they waited before going up against the enemy, they would be going down for the count. Sin can be forgiven, but the consequences may linger in the form of pain.

The sons of Israel showed up one morning on Moses' doorsteps and said:

Here we are; we have indeed sinned, but we will go up to the place where the Lord had promised.
Numbers 14:40

Moses told them it was useless because earlier they chose to undermine God. They would go into battle as underdogs and come out as dead dogs.

Do not go up, lest you be struck down before your enemies, for the Lord is not among you. For the Amalekites and the Canaanites will be there in front of you, and you will fall by the sword, inasmuch as you have turned back from following the Lord. And the Lord will not be with you.
Numbers 14:42,43

Most people want to avoid pain, and discipline is usually painful.
John C. Maxwell

If the children of Israel didn't listen the first time, why would they listen this time when Moses was very clear about the pain they would incur?

He said the Lord would not be with them because they turned their backs from following Him. Moses never even left the camp as the soldiers fought a losing battle. They paid a painful price going forward without God.

It's one thing to **hear** of pain. And it's another to **see** pain. But the ultimate pain is to **experience** pain. The pain inflicted among the Israelites could be heard, seen, and experienced.

God was very specific concerning the cost for disobedience. For every day they spied out the land, God would turn into a year. The fourteen-day journey would now turn into four weeks.

Those four weeks turned into four months. And those four months turned into four years. And those four years turned into forty years.

The Book of Numbers provides insight to the seriousness of God's displeasure with the people:

> *These are the numbered men of the sons of Israel*
> *by their fathers' households; the total of the numbered men*
> *of the camps by their armies, 603,550.*
>
> Numbers 2:32

This is the number of men of war who came out of Egypt that would die because they would not fight.

Hypothetically speaking from a mathematical point of view, that would be about 41 funerals a day for 40 years.

Think of all the pain and pitiful mourning that could be heard as women and children cried at the loss of a father, husband, son, brother or possibly all of these.

Don't see your situation as a <u>problem</u>.
See God turn it into a <u>possibility</u>.

Caleb didn't see entering the Promised Land as a problem. He saw the miracles God earlier performed to get them to the border.

Yes, there were giants, but the land was theirs for the taking. He encouraged; he explained; he extolled; he cajoled. Caleb even tore his clothes.

It was Caleb who believed the promise of God. It was Caleb who provided the positive report. But it was the ten spies that allowed the enemy to infiltrate their thinking process.

Today the enemy infiltrates your thinking and can steal the promises of God that will bring about pain due to disobedience.

> *I came that they might have life*
> *and might have it more abundantly.*
> John 10:10b

That's the last part of the verse. The first part gives an indication how a situation can disintegrate quickly and become painful.

> *The thief comes only to steal, kill, and destroy …*
> John 10:10a

THE ENEMY COMES TO <u>STEAL</u> THE REMEMBRANCES OF GOD FROM THE <u>PAST</u>.

The Israelites no longer recalled how plagues were brought upon the Egyptians. They failed to remember how the Red Sea parted into two walls so they could cross on dry ground.

Even more amazing was the children of Israel's inability to remind themselves of watching an Egyptian army of men, chariots and horses drown before their eyes.

THE ENEMY COMES TO KILL WHAT GOD HAS FOR YOU IN THE PRESENT.

He doesn't want you to experience the blessings God has for you to enjoy. The present is sometimes not lived to its fullest because we regret the past and dread the future.

THE ENEMY WANTS TO DESTROY ANY BLESSINGS OF GOD IN THE FUTURE.

Life can be experienced abundantly, but there may also be an abundance with the downside of life if we allow the enemy to come in. It may not always go in the right direction.

An earlier decision you or someone made may have caused some delays, discouragement, or even missed opportunities. Detours are sometimes part of life. Don't be dismayed.

Caleb experienced a detour during this time in his life. But there was no indication of him becoming dismayed. He remained with those who earlier didn't believe his report nor believed God would be their strength to overcome the enemy ahead of them.

For the moment it may seem as if you're going the wrong way. But you may not know if that was really the right way until you come to the end of life's journey.

The standard of measure you use to determine if you're right or wrong may be the wrong measurement.

According to society's standards, you may not be making enough money or haven't yet been promoted to the position considered for a successful career.

If you're using the family tree as a standard, those closest to you may have already nailed you to it with piercing words about their disappointment in you.

Some say they know for certain you've made wrong turns in life. You know those people and those turns because they won't let you forget nor forgive you.

The pains of life bring no pleasure. But think of the pleasure when there will be no more pain. All that you suffer on earth will be all that you'll ever suffer.

The human experience is temporary. The eternal will be the spiritual experience. That's what you want to last forever.

Pain and suffering will be no more. Love and laughter will be forever more. No one will experience loneliness or lack of love anymore. Instead, everyone will know each other the same way, a member of God's family.

Don't waste away your life by wishing it away. What you want to avoid down here may be what you'll be rewarded for up there.

God knows the trials ahead of you, but He also knows the potential treasures that could be waiting for you. Don't lose sight and don't give up the fight.

You could be worrying years off your life because of what you perceive as the wrong direction. You continually replay in your mind the time you didn't take advantage of an opportunity because you didn't consider yourself worthy at the time.

Doubts about your own decisions turn to doubts about yourself. You continually ask yourself, "What if …," because you still don't know if your decisions were right decisions.

Give yourself to make mistakes now and then,
realizing we are God's and not gods.

Les Brown

49

No matter how bad a decision you make or how long a detour you take, you can never be **so hidden** that God can't see you. That's good.

You can never be **so silent** that God can't hear you. That's even better.

You can never be **so lost** that God can lose you. That's the best.

You can never be **so far away** that God won't love you. That's the very best.

CALEB'S CREDO – THE PAIN

Caleb believed entering the Promised Land was not a problem, but a promise from God.

Caleb believed God would give him strength to overcome the enemy.

Caleb believed the delay was painful, but the time would be right when he was to take possession of the land God promised earlier.

PERSONAL CREDO – THE PAIN

I believe God's promise will trump any pain in my life.

I believe He is bigger than any giants in my mind.

I believe the enemy can no longer:
Steal the remembrance of God from the past,
Kill what God has for me in the present,
Destroy any blessings God has for me in the future.

THE POSSESSION

So look at me. The Lord has kept me alive as he promised.
It's been 45 years since Israel wandered in the desert when
the Lord made this promise to Moses. Now today I'm 85 years
old. I'm still as fit to go to war now as I was when Moses
sent me out. Now give me this mountain range
which the Lord spoke of that day ....

Joshua 14: 10-12 (GWT)

400 years was the waiting time for the children of Israel while in bondage to the Egyptians. They didn't know how long their stay would be once the sentence was pronounced.

Later they were given an additional 40 years in the wilderness upon their release due to the spies' report and bad behavior of the people because of the report.

The delay was calculated as one year for each of the 40 days the spies were scouting out the Promised Land, totaling 40 years. Very little information was available about those 40 years.

Then word came the people were being given three days before the promise would become a reality. God can use delays in life to make the necessary preparations for the next move. He knows the best way to prepare you for what He has prepared for you.

One of the most difficult things in life is the timeframe that accompanies the purpose of life. Caleb was very much aware of the timeframe with the countdown on life's clock.

Caleb was 40 years old when he was sent out by Moses as one of the spies. The penalty for the bad report delayed Caleb's promise coming true and brought about pain.

Caleb was still mentally, physically, and spiritually in shape, even after those extra 40 years, to claim his promised possession. Fast forward now and hear the orders Caleb would follow:

In three days you will cross the Jordan River and take possession of the land the Lord your God is giving you.
Joshua 1:11 (NLT)

The old warrior was about to finish out the remaining years of his life on earth; but he still had some unfinished business. Caleb approached Joshua in Gilgal and reminded him of the promise made 40 years earlier by Moses.

Aggressiveness usually diminishes with age. It increased with age for Caleb. He would not allow anything or anyone to stand in the way of God's promise—not giants or a giant mountain.

Caleb was ready to possess what was promised to him. The time was not right when he wanted to take possession. But the time was right when he finally took possession.

It was all about the timing when it came to Caleb fulfilling his calling. He was ready before the timing was right, but he had to wait for the right time.

And so it was with Jesus. He came from heaven where He was <u>above</u> time to earth where life was <u>about</u> time. How did God's plan for Jesus coincide with the preparation of Jesus?

Jesus never made a mistake or missed the direction concerning His purpose in life. The first indication of Jesus knowing His purpose was in the Temple at the age of 12-years-old.

So, what did Jesus do once He knew it? What kind of preparation did He make? Jesus didn't recruit disciples or drum up business. He went home with His family and learned a family business. He had a job. He also had a job to do. While you are waiting for God's timing, maybe you need to:

- Go home to the family
- Choose a major or a vocation
- Love your family
- Become a devoted husband/wife, son/daughter, mother/father
- Take care of daily affairs
- Take care of your aging parents

Jesus' journey to the cross took Him through a carpenter's shop. The job prepared Him for the job that God was preparing. Jesus grew in wisdom and wisdom comes through learning and living.

Many people came into Jesus' shop. This prepared Him to later come into their lives.

They told stories as Jesus listened. Later they eagerly listened to His stories.

They talked about what occupied their hearts and minds. Little did they know Jesus would later occupy their hearts and minds.

Fishermen talked about how to fish. Later fishermen listened as Jesus talked about how to be fishers of men.

Farmers told how to plant seeds in the ground. Years later, Jesus planted seeds into the hearts of others.

Shepherds talked about the lonely nights watching over the sheep. Jesus talked about being the Good Shepherd who watched over the hearts of lonely people.

Tax collectors visited Jesus' shop. They were known for what they could take from people. Jesus visited the home of a tax collector who later became known for what He gave to people. Just as it was with Jesus' timing, so it is with you.

Don't look at your job as a dead-end street. Look at it as a delay as God takes you through different and difficult jobs before you can get to your defining job.

Until then, you must be occupied with something. Jesus' life was filled with people who lived and shared their lives with Him. Look all around you and listen. God is teaching you through others, so you can eventually teach others.

Getting old is a fact of life. It begins even as we enter life. You experience it during life. You talk about it as life begins to conclude. God said it would happen. It should come as no surprise.

But it is still a surprise when it comes. No matter how much you ignore getting older, it doesn't go away. It keeps on coming. You can't do anything about getting older. But you can do something while getting older. Look at getting older as your best years approaching.

Don't keep looking back on your life as the earlier years being the "good old days." The best is yet to come.

A story is not worth reading if it stops before the final chapter. The most thrilling chapters are toward the end of the book. The highlight of a movie or a musical will crescendo before it concludes.

A life is not worth living if it ends before the Author can conclude with the final thoughts. The Book of Life has not been closed on your life because you are still living.

The Writer continues to dip the pen of life into the inkwell of purpose and writes words on your heart and thoughts into your mind. The best is yet to come.

Don't look at your age or your giants. Look at God's promises. When the opportunity presents itself, be sure you are ready to claim your mountain at any time.

You may ask yourself, "Why didn't I do that a long time ago?" "Why did it take me so long to experience this?" "Why couldn't this have happened earlier in my life?"

And the reason? God sometimes saves the best for last. That's what He did for Caleb. That may be what He is doing for you.

You can't start over in life and have a new beginning, but you can start now and have a new ending.

CALEB'S CREDO – THE POSSESSION

Caleb believed his age would not be a factor in the loss any of future benefits.

Caleb believed the time was right when he was ready to take possession of the land.

Caleb believed not anything, nor anyone could stand in the way and God had saved the best for last.

PERSONAL CREDO – THE POSSSESSION

I believe God's promise is now becoming my possession.

I believe getting older is bringing me closer to receiving God's best.

I believe God's timing is right and I will experience the promises at the right time.

I believe God has saved His best for last.

THE PERCEPTION

Today I have removed the disgrace of Egypt from you.
Joshua 5:9

The Israelites finally escaped their captivity under the Egyptians. Four hundred years in bondage and forty years in the wilderness did much to harm many people.

The children of Israel were a disgrace to other nations because of their earlier bondage to the enemy. Soon they realized it didn't matter what others thought about their past.

What mattered most was what God thought. He told them the disgrace of the past was rolled away.

God's children no longer had to carry the stigma from the past. It no longer mattered to Him. How about the others who saw it as a stain on the Israelites? Their thoughts about it didn't matter either.

As one of God's children, you may have experienced pain and suffering caused by evil in today's world. You were held captive, but finally escaped to a new walk on a new journey.

You left behind people and places where heartache and hurt were daily occurrences, but you're unable to leave behind the memories. They followed you out of your Egypt.

Your body may always have scars from the old way of living. You see permanent ink and old needle marks on your skin that will never fade away. They serve as a reminder of the old memories you tried to bury earlier.

**No one seems to be able to get over what
you did in the past. Tell them to get over it.**

The scene now shifts centuries later to the shore of Galilee after Jesus' resurrection. John 21 gives the account of Peter facing Jesus after some tragic mistakes and misdirection in Peter's life.

There was a dark side of Peter that had to be faced and an account given. Earlier Peter had three strikes called against him in a matter of hours.

Strike One: Satan manifested himself through Peter when Jesus had to address Satan while talking to Peter.

Strike Two: Peter cut off the ear of a servant when Jesus was arrested.

Strike Three: Peter denied Jesus. You're out!

Where did this leave Peter? What was he going to say to Jesus? Jesus had a meal prepared and asked about Peter's love for Him.

After breakfast Jesus asked Simon Peter, "Simon, son of John, do you love me more than these? … feed my sheep."
John 21:15 (NLT)

The first time Jesus called Peter was at the beginning of Jesus' ministry.

He told Peter, "Follow Me." Peter was a fisherman who was to become a fisher of men.

The second time Jesus called Peter once again and said, "Follow Me." Peter was now to become a shepherd and told Peter to "Feed My sheep."

The calling was the same, but the job description had changed.

The fisherman talks about the one that <u>got away</u>.
The shepherd talks about the one that <u>was found</u>.

There are three things we learn about a heavenly Father's love for you when mistakes are made, or you become misdirected:

1. **CIRCLE** → You can never get out of the circle of God's love for you.

He is the faithful God who keeps his covenant for a thousand generations and lavishes his unfailing love on those who love him and obey his commands.

Deuteronomy 7:9 (NLT)

2. **CALLING** → God's calling is still on your life.

For God's gifts and his call can never be withdrawn.

Romans 11:29 (NLT)

3. **COMPARISON** → You are to compare yourself to no one.

Peter asked Jesus, "What about him, Lord?" Jesus replied, "… what is that to you? As for you, follow me."

John 21:21,22 (NLT)

Your heavenly Father may have brought you out of a sin-strewn wasteland in your earlier life. But now you are covered by the atoning blood of Jesus Christ. You are no disgrace to the Maker of Life.

He loved you then as much as He loves you now. What is now your past was earlier your future. God saw you through those times. You made it through without knowing what you were about to go through.

It really wasn't about knowing the future that helped you make it through. It was about knowing God who knows your future.

Trust is sometimes hard to experience because of what you experienced in the past. Remember, the past is over and the future is yet to come.

There may be marks on the body from your past, but your mind no longer needs to carry those scars. God rolled away the disgrace from Egypt, and He's done the same for you.

The rest of your future is in the mind of God, so put your mind to rest. You don't need to know the future. You only need to know Him.

The future will take care of itself because God will take care of the future.

Perhaps you are frustrated by the gap that still remains between your vision and your accomplishments.

Or you may be depressed by the pages of life that are blotched with compromise, failures, betrayals, and sin.

You have had your say. Others may have had their say. But make no judgments and draw no conclusions until the scaffolding of history is stripped away and you see what it means for God to have had his say— and made you what you are called to be.

Os Guinness
The Call

THE POSTSCRIPT

Not one of the men, this evil generation, shall see the good land which I swore to give your fathers, except Caleb, the son of Jephunnah; he shall see it, and to him and to his sons I will give the land on which he has set foot because he has followed the Lord fully.
Deuteronomy 1:35, 36

Therefore Hebron became the inheritance of Caleb, the son of Jephunnah the Kenizzite until this day, because he followed the Lord God of Israel.
Joshua 14:14

You may feel a sense of failure because you've not been able to see the promise of God come true. You just can't seem to move forward. You know God has given you His promise, but you've almost given up on it and maybe even Him.

You choose where to spend the rest of your life. Sadly, most people focus their thinking on the past. Your past should not be of any interest to you anymore. You can't live it over again.

Where should your past be in your life? It's to be where it tells you. It's to be in the past. The past is part of your life that can never be changed. What happened in the **past** may be an explanation for the **present**, but it's not to be used as an excuse for the **future**.

You may become like Caleb who had only one other spy, Joshua, out of two million plus Israelites coming out of Egypt to believe there was still a promised future ahead. Caleb had a different spirit that caused him to have a different belief system.

A DIFFERENT SPIRIT CAN CAUSE YOU TO HAVE A DIFFERENT BELIEF SYSTEM.

What will it take for you to move ahead toward God's promise when you experience pain? The same thing it took for Caleb. It's a different belief system. It's called faith.

> ***And without faith it is impossible to please Him.***
> Hebrews 11:6

Faith is hard to define. It can be even harder to demonstrate. In your heart you know God is unlimited. It's in your head where you limit God. Limited faith is a result of limited thinking.

Faith is a belief that evolves into an act. Caleb's faith in God allowed him to overcome every obstacle and person that stood between God's promise and him.

God will go ahead of you, so don't get ahead of Him. While you wait for His move, you must also wait for His directions. They weren't given to the Israelites until it was time for them to make the crossing.

Be looking for your instructions during your pain to help move you on to God's promise. Instructions will be given before you go. Don't go before they're given.

Your faith can distinguish or discourage you. It's not too late to change your belief system. But it may be too late if you choose to wait.

Let's take one more final look at your past so you can move on to the future.

The four basic human needs people experience in life are to:

1. LIVE
2. LEARN
3. LOVE
4. **LEAVE A LEGACY**

Caleb certainly left a legacy that will always be remembered. Legacy is not necessary having your name written in a history book, but rather having written something on the hearts of people while living on earth.

Take a look at your life and map out how others may remember your legacy. Below is a "lifeline" where you designate certain significant events in your life that could be a part of your legacy.

Take a moment and write or draw a symbol on the line indicating certain events between the Birth and the Present.

LIFELINE:

Birth_____Present

Significant Event Samples:

Place of birth	Marriage
First love	Child(ren)
First job	Career moves
High School memories	Deaths
High School graduation	Achievements
Spiritual experiences	Disappointments

REVIEWING THE PAST:

1. Which events brought about the most positive changes in your:

Personal life?

Professional life?

2. Which events were the most difficult in your:

Personal life?

Professional life?

3. What would you do differently if you lived your life over again?

4. What would you do the same if you lived your life over again?

You've looked at life from birth to the present. Now look at it from the present until the end of your life on earth (whenever that may be).

A birthday party is being given in honor of your 85th birthday. Family, friends, co-workers and other important people in your life have gathered to pay you tribute. This could be described as your legacy.

LEAVING A LEGACY:

1. What descriptions would others use for your:

Character in life?

Attitude in life?

Priorities in life?

Relationships with others?

Reputation?

Devotion to family?

2. What characteristics would family members want to inherit?

3. What characteristics would family members NOT want to inherit?

Caleb left a legacy that will always be remembered. And his name was written in history books. There was no mistake about Caleb's calling, his purpose in life.

Many of us may never be that fortunate to be remembered in a history book. Sadly, but at times we can identify with the children of Israel who refused to take the risk of following through on the promises of God.

It pained Caleb that he had to wait for God's promise to be fulfilled in his life. But he experienced a life of no reservations, no retreats, and no regrets.

How did he move ahead when he was unable to move toward the Promised Land for so many years? Here's what you are to remember:

1. BE REMINDED

"For I know the plans I have for you," says the LORD.
"They are plans for good and not for disaster,
to give you a future and a hope."

Jeremiah 29:11 (NLT)

2. BE RELIABLE

Trust in the LORD with all your heart; do not depend upon
your own understanding. Seek his will in all you do,
and he will show you which path to take.

Proverbs 3:5,6 (NLT)

3. BE READY

…be ready in season and out of season; reprove, rebuke,
and exhort, with complete patience and teaching.

2 Timothy 4:2 (NLT)

4. BE RESILIENT

As for the rest of you, dear brothers and sisters,
never get tired of doing good.

2 Thessalonians 3:13 (NLT)

Caleb's belief system made him different. It was in the form of personal statements that were captured throughout the book as Caleb's Credo.

The following template was used throughout the book to capture a Personal Credo that provides a better understanding when processing this thing we call "life."

The seven credos can be used one at a time for each day of the week, sometimes periodically, or on an "as needed" basis. These personal belief statements will help you process God's promises that are often accompanied by pain. Read it and believe it.

DAY ONE – THE PREMISE

I believe God created me with a calling for such a time as this. He knew me before I was born and knows my pain now.

I believe God's promise is coming my way because I choose to believe in a different way.

I believe God's mercy will accompany me through the dark nights of the soul.

DAY TWO – THE PERSON

I believe God created me uniquely different with specific giftings that grant me a sense of purpose.

I believe God had a plan in mind from the very beginning before I ever had a plan in mind.

I believe God will help me overcome any obstacle that may block any opportunity He makes available.

DAY THREE - THE PROMISE

I believe my life began with a promise from God.

I believe when God takes care of me, He also takes care of my enemies.

I believe God is helping me through this wilderness experience and is moving from bondage to blessings.

DAY FOUR – THE PROCESS

I believe God has a process for each of His promises. Each process must be fulfilled for the promises to be finalized.

I believe God has a timeframe for me and He is always on time as each promise becomes a reality.

I believe God can bring about the needed miracle at this time in my life.

DAY FIVE - THE PLIGHT

I believe God's promise is on the way, even if there is a delay. I begin each day by believing.

I believe God gives me the opportunity to experience His love and blessings that make each day special.

I believe God's strength is mightier than the strength of my enemy who will experience defeat, even at this moment.

DAY SIX – THE PAIN

I believe God's promise will trump any pain in my life.

I believe He is bigger than any giants in my mind.

I believe the enemy can no longer:
  Steal the remembrance of God from the past,
  Kill what God has for me in the present,
  Destroy any blessings God has for me in the future.

DAY SEVEN – THE POSSESSION

I believe God's promise is now becoming my possession.

I believe getting older is bringing me closer to receiving God's best.

I believe God's timing is right and I will experience the promises at the right time.

I believe God has saved His best for last.

Final Thought

The Biblical account of the Promised Land entry was more about Joshua, the recognized leader at the time. Caleb could have possibly been portrayed as a tag-along due to his age and non-Jewish background. He was hoping to sneak in with no questions asked, but he didn't.

Life is influenced by the way you think and how you approach life. Many of the Israelites allowed their pain to overtake God's promise. They ultimately failed to gain entrance to the Promised Land due to disbelief, discouragement, maybe the deceit of an earlier scouting report, or eventually the denial of such a promise.

Caleb didn't become a casualty to the pain he personally experienced and witnessed. Caleb believed in God's promise that possession was a possibility.

Possessing the promise God made earlier to you is certainly a gain in life. But it can also come with pain. He knows your pain, but just as important, He knows what you will gain.

At the end of each day, be finished with it. When the evening sun slips out of sight, let the past slip out of your sight. That day is over. No longer look to the west. Turn to the east.

Look for the rising sun that will soon bring you another new day. **Anticipate it**.

That future day then turns into the present day. **Live it**.

Soon it will become a day in the past. **Forget it**.

Yesterday has been taken away. Tomorrow has not yet been given. The only way you can live life while waiting for the promise of God when pain occurs is to believe in that promise as you "faith" one day at a time.

About the Author

Ron P. Wallace graduated from Florida State University with a Bachelor of Science degree and was a starting defensive end for the Seminoles football team. He received a Master of Divinity degree from New Orleans Baptist Theological Seminary with a major in Theology and completed additional graduate work at Oxford University in Oxford, England.

Ron's ministerial background includes senior pastorates in Louisiana and Georgia. He is also a speaker at Bible conferences, retreats, revivals, and seminars. His business background includes corporate training for national corporations and governmental organizations. He also trained extensively in England and Wales. Ron's ministerial and corporate backgrounds allow him to see the mountain highs and valley lows people encounter in everyday life.

It is Ron's desire to encourage those who experience difficult trials and heartbreaks in life. He writes from personal experiences in his own life, including the tragic death of his wife, Dianne, in the midst of parenting three children. A few years later, Ron married the former Lois Jane Huddleston who experienced the death of her husband earlier in her life.

Lois Jane is a Christian singer and women's conference speaker who travels extensively throughout the United States. She has recorded over thirty projects and participated in over one thousand revivals and Bible conferences. Lois Jane is also a published songwriter. Contact information:

ronpwallace@aol.com • ronpwallace@gmail.com

www.ronwallaceministries.com • www.loisjane.com